Ghost Estate
WILLIAM WALL

salmonpoetry

Published in 2011 by
Salmon Poetry
Cliffs of Moher, County Clare, Ireland
Website: www.salmonpoetry.com
Email: info@salmonpoetry.com

ISBN 978-1-907056-70-3

COVER IMAGE: Padlock on gate © Ronfromyork | Dreamstime.com
COVER DESIGN: Siobhán Hutson
AUTHOR PHOTOGRAPH: Harry Moore – www.harrymoore.net

Salmon Poetry receives financial support from The Arts Council

For Liz

Acknowledgements

Many of the poems from this collection that have been published in print form have appeared in *The SHOp*. I am greatly indebted to the editors, John & Hilary Wakeman, for the welcome they have shown my work, as well as their kindness & friendship over the years. Other poems have appeared in: *The Forward Book of Poetry* 2010; *Other Voices Online* (othervoicespoetry.org); *The Shadowlands Project* with artist Harry Moore (harrymoore.net); *Irish Left Review* (irishleftreview.org); *The Irish Times; The Cork Literary Review* and the Upstart political poster campaign (upstart.ie). I am grateful to William Stabile, Alivento, Daniele Serafini and Giovanni Nadiani for permission to publish versions of their poems.

The Fondazione Bogliasco provided me with a fellowship & valuable space & time − not to mention new-made warm friendships − to work on the Italian poems. In particular, I am grateful for the friendship & inspiration of Grigorii Kruzhkov & for the happy hours we spent on Montale, Quasimodo & Spaziani. To him I apologise, in anticipation, for the violence I have done our beloved originals. Finally, I completed considerable work at the Princess Grace Irish Library in Monaco. I am grateful to the library, its staff and the American Ireland Foundation for the pleasure of time spent in suspension above the blue Mediterranean.

A note on the title:
The title of this collection, *Ghost Estate*, refers to the thousands of empty housing estates, partially built and sometimes occupied by a few miserable souls who made the mistake of buying their new homes on the cusp of the Irish housing bubble, just before the developers went into liquidation, and who now find themselves living alone or almost alone among hundreds of empty and decaying buildings on unfinished sites. I believe the ghost estate is a fitting metaphor for our failed republic.

Contents

In the dark times, will there also be singing?
Yes, there will be singing
About the dark times.

BERTOLT BRECHT
Motto to the 'Svendborg Poems'

Figures of speech

*To write a poem after Auschwitz is barbaric, & that corrodes
also the knowledge which expresses why it has become
impossible to write poetry today.*

   Theodor Adorno, *Prisms*, 1955

after Abu Ghraib he says
for others it was Auschwitz
what can I say
art is in the unimaginable

& nevertheless necessary
two sweet bodies lying down
the sweat the smell
naked

sated or dead
figures of speech
we say what we're told
the unsayable unsaid

we sup together
with a long spoon
we put something by
against the future

clearly apprehended
though the present is closed
& call it love
a kind of insurance

where a no-claims-bonus
costs you more
against the grievous
effigies of what we do

chains of greed
chains of fear
rendered faithfully
by standard & poor

our sentimental indices
our tectonic pain
half lamentation
half marching song

our footfall
is a rift in tenebræ
a drowned city
& all our gates

are desolate
still for tomorrow & today
silence is not enough
love is not enough

On stones

i The Rosetta Stone

things are devious.
they have that trick
of translating into various

unknown languages
we hunt for a stone to read
among the pebbles

until finally we appreciate
the pebbles
themselves are the alphabet

ii The Otolith

the ear's sea
rubs the ear-stone
to some kind of perfection
we are water where we feel
the ground

the ghost of a coelacanth
shimmers in eel-grass sensors
his movement calibrates the planet
or what we know of it

iii Slingshot

this stone
looks like the fruit
of some bleak species
there is the rind   the fruit
the pebble seeded at the heart

if we plant it in October
a stone tree will flourish
astonishing visitors
providing us
as though we needed more

with a ready supply of it
for the foreseeable future
if we collect the seed
& handle with care
we can plant a stone orchard

iv At the Neolithic copper mines

on Mount Gabriel
we found
a piece of stone that might have been
a copper miner's maul
or a piece of stone

we took it with us believing
it was not sufficiently a maul
to be defined by the act
but also capable
of the essential redefinition

in our new order
things are classified

by their mutability
by metaphor & symbol
to each according to his need

while our son went higher
& found deeper mines
of coppery water
the smelter ore
of prehistoric summers

v Deportee

if she goes home
she will be stoned to death
this simple fact
transforms the terms
there is no easy way

to think about it
we assign her
this sombre destiny
because we have forgotten
the meanings of home & stone

Ghost estate

women inherit
the ghost estate
their unborn children
play invisible games
of hide & seek
in the scaffold frames
if you lived here
you'd be home by now

they fear winter
& the missing lights
on the unmade road
& who they will get
for neighbours
if anyone comes anymore
if you lived here
you'd be home by now

the saurian cranes
& concrete mixers
the rain greying into
the hard-core
& the wind
in the empty windows
if you lived here
you'd be home by now

the heart is open plan
wired for alarm
but we never thought
we'd end like this
the whole country
a builder's tip
if you lived here
you'd be home by now

it's all over now
but to fill the holes
nowhere to go
& out on the edge
where the boys drive
too fast for the road
that old sign says
first phase sold out

A hundred keys at our door

a hundred keys at our door
the sycamore has been
in the wars
where are the refugees

who tried to unlock
our hearts
this storm from the west
large in the trees

a noise
as big as war
I'm talking
about winter

at this time of year
& already I worry
about tidal surges
& the memory

of father   mother
sitting by the fire
seawater lapping the legs
of the kitchen chairs

In memoriam David Marcus

*In the blink of an eye we went from broken windows
to death camps.*

    Unknown Rabbi

i *In the blink of an eye*

glass in the air
a heartbeat
to let things settle
we closed our eyes

there were chimneys
in the dust
& railroad tracks
commonplace things

we swept the street
ordered glass & worried
about the future
as we do now

ii *Jewish graveyard, wintry light*

down in the valley
they are lighting fires
the smoke follows
the lie of the land
everything is slightly uncertain
in a certain light

who listens to eulogies
though they may be well done
& occasionally necessary

we are asked to remember the dead
by every stone in the road

iii *You curse your memory*

we all have bad memories
at least a century of them
friends lost
bad days bad dreams

the heart as stone
fanatical
bits & pieces
too carefully assembled

hope is the hardest thing
to recall
days at the piano
Mozart escaping as usual

that story
read at a sitting
(fulfilling the fourth unity
according to Poe)

so perfect you wept
you forget who now
his first his very first
writing because there's nothing

left to do
hopefully
something about the Shoah
your cursed memory

The news is

the news is a seventy percent eclipse
as bad as we can expect & probably
one of His more measured verdicts

the news is three nestlings
died of a sudden microwinter
we found their airtex corpses on the lawn

the news is the world is warming up
we get grapes & olives & they get desert
but our garden died in the summer of 06

& Dublin ran out of water & it was too hot
to keep the windows closed on the road west
even in the shade of the old viaduct

where a long time ago before global warming
a young man hanged himself in despair
from what was left of the permanent way

Urchin

i

the grey green stone
was not a stone
an old sea-urchin
maybe a billion years ago
whose body exchanged itself
for silica
a fossil
disguised
by this stony shore
under my boot
it makes no excuses now
its slow betrayal of self
is shameless

ii

a snow of creatures
toy bones
dissolving & resolving
the milky ocean
settling in drifts
the taste of time
is chalk in the mouth

iii

I never consider
the meaning of love
knowing
is less important
than being
& feeling

I never trust oracles
although they alone
may understand
time's settlement

iv

minus its spines
there is still
the chalk test
the heart urchin
in the sea of chalk
the fiddle heart
the hedgehog
the stilt-walker
the old hunchback
the mud-gobbler
the bed-burrower
the bottom goblin

v

still a stony weight
that fits my hand
like a vestigial bone
still somehow
true to itself
& not itself
I admire
its reticence
never write anything down
my mother said
give them nothing
this urchin
in his corbelled head
knows silence

vi

prophets of doom
soothsayers & naysayers
the augur
burrowing out of sight
seeing & saying
but never hearing
the world
dissolve in ashes
the midnight of love
the first light of silence
the day of the urchin
in the hegemony of stone

vii

the still comforting
familiar urchin
a child's head
surfacing
wave-combed
striated
radiant
he waves
& his mother
signals time
it's time to go
nobody knows
what will become of us
on this wordless shore
I see her standing
at the water
in glassy evening light
& I dive
time after time
for a sea-urchin shell
in the sand at my feet

Making old bones

the neighbours' dogs
bury their dead in our garden
I see them hunting out the bones
from behind the half-barrel
& under the rosemary
the way retrievers do
nothing forgotten is lost

a sign says *famine graveyard*
pointing to a place
we thought was our own
though we cannot say the name
(Srebrenica? Kibuye?)
with any certainty
we identify the clothing

a little shamefaced at the state it's in
& a tibia in the parsley
a bad hand of phalanges
metatarsals beyond the clothes-line
a hamletful of skulls
whose faces we can't recall
the wind sings in their eyes

pouring down the Maglin valley
from Ladakh in Kashmir
to the line of control
we walk out the frozen road
with the little we can save
depending on the charity of dogs
who bury their bones in our memory

from Guardrail

after the Romagnolo of Giovanni Nadiani

we don't know the why of it
& no-one remembers
the day & which of us
first got it into his head
but every night bang on nine–fifty
we stop playing
turn our cards face down on the table
& we don't care
if someone messes with them
& we get out of the café

we turn our faces to the sky
in the last rays of the sun
& we all want to be first to see
the hiccuping of the lights
of the Ryanair flight
coming in from London Stansted
to land in Forlì
at the foot of Bertinoro

no–one speaks
we are watching the big bird
slowly slowly coming
thinking of those people inside
& we are melancholy for no good reason
maybe for all those stories
over our heads
wandering the face of the world
or maybe only for us
who have never been anywhere
so when we decide to fly ourselves
in our own planes

with a lump in our throats
it will be forever
with no one to remember us

*

we only want
to stay here a little longer
on this Sunday afternoon
brushed by the breeze
which is coming & going
sitting in bare feet
stretched on the grass
looking up
at the slow pale clouds
crossing one by one
the dark blue of our thoughts.
feeling this warm breeze
closing our eyes
& the weariness of our days
leaching from our bones
& for once deceiving ourselves
it will be the same
also on that day
with the wind
sighing in the dust
to scatter us lightly
in another world

*

we who lean against the walls
beaten by the afternoon sun
to keep our necks
from the bitter mistral
hands frozen in our pockets
jiggling the few bob

we who already feel
that no sun can hold
against the hail
that before we even know it
will soak us through
completely riddled
only round the corner from home

*

we who keep the windows down
tearing round the orbital
we never notice
the thorns are in flower

that scent for a second
is in our noses
& we're drunk on it
so it turns our heads
beyond the steel guardrail
& we don't know
where it comes from
only we half-remember
when we were kids
an evening in May
barefoot by the river

& so it seems to us
that life
is all there
in that scent
we still have in the nose
though we no longer know
where it came from

Flight

for Rui Zink

I missed the flight
because of the terror alert
that has terrified everyone

I had some liquid in my pocket
that they thought
might be explosive

just the artificial tears
I have begun to use
because they come easier

& less painfully
& while I waited for my tears
to be decommissioned

the other passengers said
who would think of taking
tears on a journey

during the war on terror
& where did I think I was going
& who would I use them on

Our Icarus

he is our Icarus
our sunstruck
cosmonaut
taunting the gods
on our behalf
a shadow
in the sun's face
so we all come out
to see the collapse
the screaming drop
though we might
at least have thought
about the flight
we take photographs
of the crash site
& souvenir feathers
our children ought
to be impressed
that we attend his death

What is unacceptable about dreams

for Illan

is not the terror we feel
but that we create them

that the twin towers meant first
the globalist dream

& only later humanity
& people who were falling not flying

this is the terror we fear
that we dreamed of the falling tower

Job in Heathrow

i

with the frightened crowd
for whom every new alarum
is an authority
queuing in drifts
between levels
the so-called waiting lounges
of the so-called world

the word is out
there are bombs
in the whiskey
no carry on
this is the last straw

& nervous people
& nervous men in stab vests
& nervous men in puffa jackets
& no smoking signs
& this is a silent airport
you pay the man
& you wait for a sign
there the prisoners rest together
the small & great are there
studying departures
in a state of heightened alert
code somewhere close to titian

a man holds his woman in his arms
& another watches the door expectantly
& the enemy comes on his own feet to his grave
we are a trifle unsettled
we think about sodoku & the crossword
as though minding minutiae

the universe will look after itself
this is the world as it is *habibi*
it's all we know
try to step off
& the man will bring you down

ii

master I cried
who are these bastards
do we have any idea who these people are
willowy women in Gucci shoes
men in silk leather jackets
they circulate freely
in the recycled air
must we do homage
or will a simple nod be enough
a greeting *ex gratia*
do they expect to be questioned
to assist enquiries
interrogation
water-boarding even
look here comes one crying
hopeless hopeless hopeless
& are we supposed to sympathise
when the gentry find themselves in the same boat
or plane
as everyone else
or at least in the same lounge
love brought her down she says
according to her biography
it was a chance encounter at a drug-fuelled orgy
in somebody somebody's motor yacht
the coke blew her away
blew her brains away
& opened her legs
& wore her sinovial membrane down
it all sounds a little hollow now

with the end of the world upon us
& bombs in the whiskey
love love love she says
so much for all you need is love

iii

they come & go like cranes
restless creatures look
& their pale limbs against the azure sky

I see myself in you
a sly oriental craft
sails on the water

& are we supposed to sympathise
& who are these people
extra-communitari

there in the upper circle
the automatic doors
are automatic from the outside only

we see them as it were through a tinted glass
wringing their hands
begging admission

these troublesome ghosts
what was it Marx said in the famous opening
something haunting

a man had his left hand chopped off
for with it he slew his master
& he begged a pipe of tobacco

& then he died
the ultimate manumission
in those days they knew their place

he was a slave & his place of execution
is here
upon this fatal shore or landing

at least Virginia apologised
they come & go like cranes
restless creatures look

& they make their homes in marsh & useless ground
& leave when they can
those Turks Hector & Heraclites

& Euclid the Egyptian
Pythagoras the fundamentalist
& all the gang

Avicenna the metaphysician
thinking about his credentials
they don't let Uzbekistanis operate on Christians

even in Hell
someone is tuning up
old Ali Farka Touré on the air guitar

a session
come on boys
when did you make a run for it

no running here
cancer of the bones
death comes like ice

the heart of the moon
where you come from they get that
on a bad day as I remember

iv

& somebody says the loo is blocked
dear god
what will they think of next
they've closed off the last line of escape
another safety valve
what will become of us

my father gave me Marcus Aurelius
on the last day of my holidays
& the old emperor stood me in good stead you know
communing with himself

at Gallipoli
we ran our ship ashore into the sand
we saw tesseræ in the parados
& I said to my sub I said

six or seven thousand years of this
& here we are again attacking the Turks
will it never end
meaning we the philhellenes

& that idiot Bean
is that a light I see on Tenedos
I'm dying for a smoke dear boy
& I'm too old for this

a decent education makes it all worthwhile
knowing what we know et cetera
this one is a beauty
see how he walks

don't you love an Arab
oh the Sheik of Araby
if I don't take a leak
I shall leak

& my sub said to me
an ignorant child
it's all this Allah business sir
that gets to me

v

that girl bled to death
a million tiny wounds
& everyone said how well she looked
jammed against the partition
her pants still around her knees
a note of caution
peace accursed woolf
or words to that effect
they would not give her the last rites
the blacksuit serpents
mal dare e mal tener
they look after their own
but she is a beauty no mistake
they eat each other
round & round they go
her state is blessed
out of this world at least
poor child
they direct the almighty guns
against self-harmers
she was my daughter
your daughter too

vi

the guards wear sunglasses
a society of spectacles as the man said
like the dark ground of a cameo
except in reverse
their faces are blanked by their eyes
if someone farts we're dead
see their trigger fingers
& the somnolent insouciance
of the human face
if we had an air force
we would send you bombers

for I do not know whose voice is crying
when I cry
never look back at the border
the furies follow behind
never poke fire with a knife
never piss into the sun
abstain from beans
these few precepts mark you well
what of the isles of the blest
not for us my son
not our kind

they look at us
& we look at them
there's bush that vicious mole
another non-statement
of what he thinks
another good one about axes
or the coalition of the willing
not the coerced
do we have to have TV everywhere
fly sky news news sky fly
oh for a universal remote

please note the automatic doors
are no longer automatic
access to the open areas is restricted
arrivals is closed
all unattended baggage will be destroyed
nervous people
will be arrested
please note
the contrapuntal strains
of childhood & exile
we are all strangers in one sense or another
depending on each other

vii

our children are hungry
they look up
& are not fed
not even a complimentary coke
the cost of living
higher than expected
year on year increases
sometimes out of reach
never easy to make ends meet
but what can you do
the grey wolf
walks the steppes of the heart
every father
every mother
knows the sound of his passing
his fierce eyes
but one day you must let go
you just let go

viii

I said you should eat your garlic
it's good for digestion
& indicated in these cases
but you made a pig of yourself
friend Elpenor
you were pissed
when you fell from that roof
a troublesome shade
don't you look at me like that

out on that headland
the wind whistling in our drawers
remember the fire we burned
you kindled up quick enough
bare flesh & bread & young dark wine
once is enough for anyone
once & for all
but I did it twice
that was the kind I was
until the going down of the sun
when all the ways grew dark
& the sea was dark
& dark-prowed ships moved on it
let go let go I said
& we pulled out of that place
on our travels
what fun we had
at the mercy of the wind
wherever our fancy took us

we querulous ghosts
this is our ancient future
this holding bay
this waiting room
where no room awaits
this offing

this roadstead
this glass hole in the horizon
we could be flying
& instead we're falling
out of the world & into the air
life is ticketless
point to point
& then there is Costa Coffee
& fear

ix

how do you feel my dear
stricken at heart
but you're on television
smile
I am stricken at heart
& losing the sight of my eyes
no flocks of sheep nor ploughed-land
saw I
but a barren wilderness
I am stricken at heart
o desolate men
let us hide our faces
sighing & whispering
in this place of tears
nor law nor council
but everyone in his own place
alone

there was abundant flesh
& so called consumer durables
& we looked at the sun's single eye
& saw the travel brochure
& thought why not
it was a hole

promiscuous death
no rights knows
never tell them your real name
say I am no one or someone
anyone
but whom I am

x

that man is a renowned poet
see his hair
the thinking man's easy answer
impounded
in this nether crib
after Adorno said that business about poetry
how can the man dare
never mind this or that holocaust
I say
better yet
think about holocausts
as something people did
a long time ago
& are inclined to do
once in a while
take the long view
politics makes you strident
which is bad news for the poet
whatever way you think about it
silence
is the only answer
& nothing comes of that
so twitter on
fiddle even
at least we're occupied

xi

& for his simple heart
I loved him
three days he was dying
it was past all tragedy
& we were eating & drinking
like there was no tomorrow
sorrow takes you that way
rain cleared after midnight
& the tide came in
all the small sounds
of the drowning foreshore
sea-creatures coming home
& land-creatures fleeing
& he drowned I suppose
it certainly sounded like that
a man who looked out on the sea
all his life
but a landsman really
not overly privileged by death

xii

I look up & there is glass
or maybe sky
summer clouds
brittle & bare
& I think Mr Death how do you do
this bubble of blue
when the sky falls
all we ask for is plausible deniability
our travelling companions
our ancient kinship
consanguinity
I will deny everything three times
how we die matters less than why
or so they say
but if there is an easy way out

xiii

we are inclined to confidences
as the light fades
& calling to mind the distant past
& places we will never see again
departures are cancelled
someone says
when they let us smoke it's the end
& pret-a-manger is running out
but we never despair
which is how we won the war

the game involves numbers
& knowing their place
the so-called biometric data
we're looking for coherence
not meaning
competing against ourselves

we sense
things coming together
a great clandestine gathering
something that happens elsewhere

anything to keep the nights at bay
I get anxiety
a heightened state of alert
xanax is what I get
we're just fading aren't we
we're looking at the twilight
oh yes
fading

Over the gantries

a broken sky
like the rotten silver
of an old mirror
so much is lost in the telling
I hear the day shift walking
the night-shift winding down
accidents will happen
the pressure is immense

between one shift & the next
entropy gains access
& a man dies in the process
if I knew his name
I would tell it now
unknown soldiers
die for the shareholders
the sky never changes
& nothing shakes the dividend

The isogloss of silence

east of this line
there is no word for no
denial is not an option
the land of truth let's say

north of this line
there is no word for yes
everything happens by accident
the land of nay let's say

south of this line
there is no word for tomorrow
the present is forever
the land of the libertines let's say

west of this line
there is no word for east
they think they are alone
the land of the spectacle let's say

only there
in that middling patch of land
you can say anything
if you have a mind to

but we haven't
heard from them
in a very long time
& the last word we had was silence

What will become of our children

what will become of our children
whose teachers no longer read
who play games with their fingertips
when every knock at the door is a blow
& the laws of hospitality have been indefinitely suspended
when the news is more exciting than the cartoons
when things are either ours or evil

& reality TV is reality TV
& all kinds of intelligence are unreliable
except counter-intelligence
& everyone's dream is possible
& there is no such thing as impossible
except that space is something
their grandparents had
an impossible dream even for spacemen now

We imagine the police

we imagine the police
cameras catching other people
doing things that irritate us
in their cars
this is the police state
of mind
& we are sensible citizens
of the commonsense
as we shop in the late evening
in the supermarket
that never closes
not even for God
& we try to remember what we want
& we try to buy only what we need
& desire keeps getting in the way
we genuflect
before other people's shopping
in aisles sacred
to the memory of home
cooking & detergent
& the kind of things your mother baked
& as we are occasionally electrocuted
by the metal
we begin to believe
that bread belongs to today
that there are different qualities of white
that there are no preservatives
that the meat
is prime
& the supermarket cares for us
& that every little helps
it is chip & pin
in the late evening
under the watchful eyes
we imagine
people using our cards

to buy things we would never buy
in places we have never been
on a day or days
without our express
permission
this is the police state
of mind
as we drive home in the night
with a car full of things
we scarcely believe are real
our past haunted by
kitchen paper rolls
cans of asparagus tips
stick & click LED lights
mosquito candles in case
we get global warming soon
disposable barbecues
fruit psychosis
& probiotic yoghurt
& canned salmonella
& thawing petits-pois
& lawn weed 'n' feed
& a nest box
& a special kind of notepaper
that has forget-me-nots
& a memory stick
& a device for opening
reluctant cardboard cartons
& a fold up tent
for when we fold our tent
& a wallet-full of promises
that there will still be shopping
no matter how dark the time

The property developer's wet dream

I dreamed I was
driving a kompressor
through amberley
ashley
hazeldene
kenley
berkeley
willowmere
castletreasure
. bellevue
heather lawn
heather crescent
ashley mount
hunter's way
kingsway
welwyn way
the paddocks
hazelmere close
wyndham close
ashley close
oh
brierly
kensington downs
endsleigh

Armageddon Sunday morning

& to the angel of the church in Pergamos write; These things
saith he which hath the sharp sword with two edges

King James Version, *Revelation*, 2.12

I dream of the collapse
of everything we hold dear
probably on a Sunday morning
things will just stop

the last man will walk
the suburbs
on feet of brass
& will be defeated

by the commonplace light
the toys   the wet cars
the frying bacon smell
the privacy

& no one will write
to Ephesus or Pergamos
where there are angels
all that old stuff

for we have been eating
the future & selling
the past & our children
are gone to hell on skates

& a black horse follows them
something out of the ordinary
& his hooves smoke
where they touch the street

In Forlì I dreamed

for Adele D'Arcangelo

in Forlì I dreamed
that they made my bed
of all the things that Europe did
blood & the dead
stony futures
torture loss
I dreamed
I woke in pain
& all my friends were there
I said
this is the bed that Europe made
the worst bed in the world
why me

& someone said
everyone sleeps here once
count yourself lucky
that it came to you
on such a night as this
the moon on the campanile
the cloisters & the wine
while we were here in Forlì
& I slept again
& dreamed some other dream
now gone
& woke in the morning early
cold

Poem on the anniversary of Gramsci's death

we are free texts
the billboard says to me
I say you never heard
of Antonio Gramsci

Letter to a doctor

for William Stabile

they put a camera up my ass
they put a camera down my throat
(not the same camera)
(or not the same day)
they made pictures of my brain
in onion skin
my spinal column
(intact I'm glad to say)
my heart in hologram
dear doctor
what else is there

I think
I eat .
(I think I eat)
(I eat I think)
what goes in comes out
more or less on cue
I overheat at times
that's the way the world goes
although I have never been
exactly straight
I am approximately upright
& things that happen in my head
have their correlative elsewhere

you & I are transiting
the great digestive tract
that is the world
dear doctor
we all become much
the same stuff

& shadow
& when it all comes down
you can know too much

since there never was a Jesus Christ
as per the label
there is no such thing
as the perfect life
no let there be light
no logos to speak about
no way out
the world is everything
that is the case
so let's call it even-stevens doctor
let's say
for the sake of argument
I have discharged myself
what then

While there was nothing

they checked him over for any
removable prosthetics
false teeth   hearing aids   contact lenses
then inserting no more than
a thin piece of plastic
into his last good vein
they erased his wife & children
an examined life
a lot of William Shakespeare
& sundry others
& for a brief period there was

nothing

we are the story of our lives
a more or less consistent narrative
& yet when he woke up
he had not been
in any accepted sense
a dead man
& everyone was pleased
that everything that happened
while there was nothing
had gone so well

Celebrating with cigars

there are no matches
no fire
we try to light them on the cooker
but the hob is dodgy
we try tinder
& the two sticks business
& search for a flint
though the house is built on sand
we run a wire from plus to earth
hoping for a glow
& throw the switch
& all the lights go out
finally we accept
there is nothing to celebrate
& anyway
there are no cigars

The sexuality of women in cinemas

for Mick Hannigan

they are attentive
but not to me
their hair trembles
at the touch of light
like a field
of gossamer
their steel shoulders
tentative

packets rustle
but not skirts
not plackets
their touch-screen lips
their sympathy
they are transported
abandoning themselves
but not to me

Mother & child

she unpicked the seam
the collar opening to reveal
dust & dandruff
a kind of lint
like a bandage

then she turned it
the needle flying flying
visible invisible
the stitch she learned as a girl
as a seamstress

all the while
in another room
he plies the needle
to a different end
the seam is never turned

to invent is to remember
in his dream
his mother opens the seam
shakes out the dust
& wraps him in the lint

Child

she stands at the very edge
of the known
where falling is pleasure
& standing still
is going back
a breath of wind on her
trembling skin
or her mother's distant call
in the perfect synchrony of now
& the fall begins
now she makes her own
rising gale
the hurry of going down

Dark matter

he contained more matter
than can be accounted for
without him the mass
of the universe is impossible
the hole in your heart boy

into the dark fell
women & animals
grace & pardon
love & affection

on a black night
his invisible face was a light
a new calculus
where nothing mattered

I saw him yesterday
hunched in the doorway
of Square Deal
a bottle of sherry
in a brown paper bag
his face closed to the west
that day's dying sun

Fast asleep

night is no fastness
the siege machines on a thundery plain
far below
nor impotent nor swift to fall

I dreamed of my mother last night
her mouth gagged
still she said come into my coffin
I kissed her wet cheek

Death enters by the back door

death enters by the back door
a quiet person
in a dusty apron
no fuss no ceremony
no glamour

& also I see her
arms full of daffodils
from the hill field
waving to me
her voice a bell

My mother

waiting for me
to emerge
a half-man
from the submarine world
to be enclosed
by her arms
in a towel that said
Benner's Hotel

& behind her
barley ripens
a man
who is my father
lifts the ear
to his mouth
he knows
when the time
is right

but waving & calling
I remember
& later
my father's sleep
invaded by sand

pale august
light in the eyes
light as ash as time
that seaborne light
the ice-blink
of what is gone
forever
an invisible line
the event horizon
of the apocalypse
of never again

In Galileo's telescope I see

for Alessandra Natale

in Galileo's telescope I see
not clearly
not very far
something already encountered
an old man with white hair
poor eyes
poor eyes
feeble & tearful & full of memory
& he is myself as much as my father
after the main burst & flooded
in his head

he stares back at my unblinking eye
as if at the future of the universe
the dying sun
the folding galaxies
the going out of everything & the stars
going down into blindness
& not once
does he look away

this is the tragedy of my father & maybe mine
that he looked unblinkingly & inconsolably
into tomorrow
& tomorrow night

in Galileo's telescope I see
another country
not very far
from which today is the indelible future
& another child's yesterday
& so on in the glass
lens upon lens
toward the vanishing point

My mother's keys

my mother's keys are in a bag
I am afraid to open
the key to the locked drawer
where we kept the takings
bank books
the float

the keys of the shop
in the cold clear seaside mornings
a sticky yale & a deadlock
the smell of wet seaweed
the keys of the house
& certain unknown keys

to the past
or the future
possibly the key to everything
blackening in there
like the others in every way

I am afraid in case
opening the bag might bring
all the usual consequences
for mythical containers
everyone knows
wishing is a dangerous activity

for we may get what we wish for
but not what we want
& yet I wish on this bright morning
for a key to a PO Box
that I could put a note in

Flying towards a funeral

our imaginations
are terrestrial
at 40,000 feet we feel
we could navigate by the clouds
that everything would still
be there tomorrow
if we came back

we are flying on the edge
of what is happening
& it is possible to look
at the window
& imagine ourselves not there
no longer taking part
not flying towards
a funeral

but in this time not our own
this air not of the air
this cumulus of grief
this near miss in time
we feel temporary
& too late
our time of arrival
already later than
your departure

Clearing my aunt's house
after the funeral

someone here
was a collector
of keys
a hundred years
of them
the doors gone
a thousand outsides
& no inside

After Brecht

for twenty years
it was winter
o death send
embassies
do not look her
in the face
one day
in spring
she died
& we found
the body
of a child

Passage

from the Italian of Alivento

when I cry
I cry for my days
my always flying time

between happenings
when breathing
becomes a white wing

I think
son of a woman
mother of a man

the written jingle
of repeated farewells
until the last estrangement

the door closed
the mouth of the delta
of the dead

I have a mad tongue

I have a mad tongue on me
you have a heart of gold
she had a mind to marry me
I had an eye for her kind

she had those blue eyes
we had a good time
while we were having it
I had a girl in every port

like the dog I had my day
I have a pain where
I never had a window
I have cancer of the bowel

they had me opened & closed
I have it on good authority
I have six months at best
they haven't the heart to tell me

I have a desperate thirst
I have a bottle of the quare stuff
I have two glasses on the sideboard
you have a heart of gold

The Christ of Velasquez

for Gerry Murphy

I see a dead man nailed
to a plank
someone knifed him
& stole his shorts

Discourse

for Liz

is what the dogs in the street know
but we don't
until it's too late

Election 2007

the thieves
exchange bodies,
twins from opposite sides

the party of up
the party of down
like quarks

'A play before mourners'

– Walter Benjamin on Tragedy

I can never see without remembering
out in the open fields
where the fieldmouse sleeps
where the hare warms his sett of wound grass
where the hawk shivers
where the skaldcrow waits to pick up the pieces
life is a play before mourners
Lear is my father's memory

I can never walk without falling
the edge of the ocean
whispers about belonging
the seal watches from big dark eyes
the gannet dives into blindness
we all go down into the same dark
life is a play before mourners
Lear is my father's memory

I can never stand without pain
& my bones age before me
who will say this is the wrong grave
who will say this is a mistake
they buried the wrong man
in my father's grave
life is a play before mourners
Lear is my father's memory

Drowned oboe

after the Italian of Salvatore Quasimodo

rapacious pain your gift
in this late hour

a frozen oboe counting over
& forgetting
immortal notes not mine

in me it's evening
the sunset water
on my sea-grass hands

great wings in a faint sky shimmer
the heart migrates
& I am empty

& my days wreck here.

The chronicles of the nettle

after the Italian of Maria Luisa Spaziani

the white roofs not snow but
dust or lime or flour
here in the interstices of the tiles
the nettles salute me

my emblem my tsarina
a rose refuses to grow there
neither lily nor acacia
violet nor tuberose

as in a game my warrior
shall we inaugurate
a new convention
a new mythology

The transplant

under our striped quilt
you are sleeping
your head off
no one has
perfected the art
of head transplant
I should wake you
while there is still time
I love your sleepy head

When I go

I will go in the head
I will land on the roof
& stalk the cat with the swifts ·

the beech hedge has wafers of copper
too many of them
spring's disused viaticum

poetry is noticing
& the invention of new ways
of making friends

I am crazy with you
after thirty years of
of more of the same

I dance in your disordered dreams
making sleeping arrangements
that will not work

organising vegetable unions
talking the dogs down
offering opportunities

when I go I go in the head
I sit on my haunches
defying gravity to do its worst

I dream you are a high tide
at half past six
I come in with the coffee

The house of the customs men

after the Italian of Eugenio Montale

you do not recall the old custom-house
on the cliff tilted above the rocks
desolate it waits for you since
the evening you went in & your
restless thoughts hived there

a southwesterly beats the old walls
& your smile has lost its lightness
the compass swings wildly
& the dice fall against us
you do not remember   old times
turn your thought aside   a tangled thread

I still hold the beginning of it but the house
recedes & the smoky weathervane
on the roof's ridge turns ruthlessly
I hold the beginning but you are still alone
not even breathing in the darkness

oh the fugue of the horizon where
occasionally a tanker lights the night
is there safe passage here (yet the reef-foot
teems with broken water...) you do not
remember the house of this particular evening
& I no longer know who goes or stays

Drawn blind

In memoriam Bessie Kirwan

i *Drawn blind*

she stands at the drawn blind
the way she used to stand

looking out on the light
she thinks is a bright dawn

the sheer golden light
that floods her sandy eyes

the luminous
unknowable outside

(& the day tries for rain
behind the drawn blind)

ii *Evening: light fading*

when my eyes are dark
but I can feel the daylight
still almost there
I see people

shapes that come towards me & smile
wearing my mother's gingham dress
the last one she bought

& wonderful patterns appear
that I know are not there

iii   The grace of light

after the Italian of Daniele Serafini

a still pale sea brings
to slothful nostrils
the birth of morning

disclosing to this human form
the grace of the light
that undoes present time

Spiders

this is the time
when spiders build
their neurotic bridges

I hesitate to unsettle them
five times stronger than steel
cable laid

of invisible strands
truer than poetry
stronger than song

than love than light
still they tremble
they are unreasonable

& though they stay the corners
of my house
prevent the light

from oscillating
warn of emptiness
beyond the back step

steady the plates
upon which everything depends
as far as the continental shelf

& deliver me
from rash bluebottles
they do not believe

in themselves
those faithless anorexics
those hopelessly retiring cornerboys

I have never known a time
when their hawsers
did not shiver

in the pearly morning
sometimes an exchange
so tactful as to be insensible

to the naked eye
of energy or fear
between air & form

sometimes
grappled to light
waiting above my head

like exploded toys
or nano-weapons
or a surgical device

& times I think
these tiny cantilevered stanzas
are declaratory

the fragile sign
of intelligent design
a subtle anathema

against sceptics
or reason enough
for something instead of nothing

Hedgehog

this is the time
when hedgehogs
snuffle in nightdress
for slugs
or beer
or woodlice
prickly footballs
the dog rolls
their crake
is saurian
we found one
sniffing crisps
in a crisp-bag
the salt-addict
of the spine clan
we saw one
stalking the lawn
on his own ground-plan
demanding harmony
with menaces
the phantom beetler
the hunter gatherer
the awkward customer
the morning star
the hedge-urchin
all points & purpose
& once we found
one asleep
in a compost heap
innocence itself
a stash
of hypodermics
in a jute sack

Something there is that does not love a wall

i

but we build this wall of wood together
contra winter's gales
& tumbler cats
facing out
the trace of terrible winters
in tree rings
summer's thickening bark
like building our own skin
to keep our hearts warm
a hull
for hearts of beech

& make a boatyard
or a farmyard
of our suburban lawn
the resin smell
the saw-tooth
like a maker's mark in the bark
we are doing a good thing
an ark
to house the roofless
spiders woodlice hedgehogs
husbanding fire
to spite the endless rain
in the biblical days
of late November
the kind of thing our fathers said
I hear mine at my shoulder
slope it in
turn the bark-side up
to keep the weather out
our tumblehome
our barque
our ship of fools

ii

we use the property pages
to start the fire
the best of kindling
billionaire houses
giving up
calorific value
all that negative equity
going up in smoke

we burn their woods
their gates
their pool-covers
their beech-wood hedge
their garden seats
what of their concrete
armless aphrodites
boyish pissers
spouting dolphins

nothing escapes
the conflagration
winter is fire
in our smoky valley
we contemplate
the ignis fatuus
of twenty years
with equanimity
& the dog sleeps
with his nose to it

iii

we're burning
the furniture
the walls
the boards
the skirting
rafters soffets noggins
& the ties
in the invisible house
we are about to see
blue sky fresh air
a horizon of sorts
a version
of the future
that is not the past
bigger than commonsense

though we have burned
away the rain
& a hole in the world
directly above our heads
lets the stars in
not everything goes

a wishbone in the ash proves
that wishes
are impervious to fire
though the breast is not
where hope propagates
like poppy-seeds
red flags waving
on every waste

Eight observations about hope

i

the empty island houses
look to the sound
& there are two doors

one to the east where
morning is gold silver or lead
according to prophecy

& one to the west
in case its long unhappy day
should ever end

ii

early one morning
I saw
in the interior of a wave
a shoal of mackerel
afterwards the usual
morning sea

but the inside
was alive & the fish
turned in it
as though it were
all that existed
& with the clean grace

of something
that imagined itself
in command
of its element

iii

nature loves to hide
I turn the sleeping dog
& a ball of maggots
clings to his side

& now I see
his eyes are not
glaring at me
& the maggots

too are blind
or paranoid
everything they feel
is internalised

iv

a blackbird dips his head
& retracts
caught
in the brazen beak
the reluctant worm

the worm holds
to the idea
of subterfuge
a posteriori
like a philosopher
clinging
to his first insight

v

the beeches
aspire to light
time is running out

& the last leaves
wait out the fog
hoping for one more go

the radio expects
a clearance later
then gales on all coasts

dawn is a minor
difference of opinion
about letting the dog out

vi

a cloud is a full fish
in the sky today
a mackerel in negative
against a red sea

they may cover it with iron
& be grateful for it
but once the sun sets
a cloud is a cloud

the moon knows
the factories are gone home to tea
the shops & the traffic
just sleeping round

metaphor drops dead
about half past four of a winter's night
concrete comes in
with the night shift

we inhabit the unfinished site
inventing plans
in retrospect matching the fake trees
to the artist's impression

vii

a flight of crows
out of a stubble field
a wintry sunset

the crows are a pattern
the field inhabits

twilight
silence
fade to black

viii

I start with black
hoping for light
an easy time
hoping for quotas
for upper limits

the day without pain
not the pain without day

at this time of year
the dawn is late
it will be welcome
when it comes

'Black ice'

2 films by Stan Brackhage

i 'Black ice'

I slow it down
frame to frame
hunting that
elusive white
& realise
this is the night
coming at me
in the headlights
the colour of time
slipping away
blood & spilled wine
& the night sky
just before dawn
& the ocean
out beyond
the continental shelf
& remote places
where animals
have never seen
a person
& that person's
indigo eye
glimpsed through
the ice in a glass

ii 'The Dante Quartet'

hell begins badly
darkening swirls
of blood & ink
a terrible angel
& some sort of force
like a cyclone
in India ink
a sky full of mistakes
beyond redemption
a squid
a man approaching
or at least a manshape
across rough water

& then there are
places that look
like home
a low distant shore
faces as of friends
& casual acquaintances
happy days
become painful memories
in the accelerating
tulip petals

The cripple at the bacon

the cripple at the bacon
exhibition
saw himself repeated
x times ten

so he never saw george dyer
or bacon
or henrietta moraes
or the attendant

or the child pushing
a doll's pram
who took him full on
pitching him

into figure
in a mountain
landscape never triggering
the alarm

so when we tried
to help
it was too late
to prevent

his cartoon
fall through
a mountain
gorge

ending in silence
at the vanishing point
his home from home
he may be watching us now

In the museums

i

the fish live
in the fish museum
in the basement
in perfect light
almost touching
our world
not looking at us
purposeful
circulating
in the fake sea
like a cocktail party

& nothing unnatural
happens beyond
the glass wall
in the disneyland
of happy fish
interspecies sex
or cannibalism
or insider trading
the fish will never
unite against us

& we strike
a bourgeois pose
in the submarine space
between the street
& the seabed
glass is our police
the difference
between us
frail as a leaded light

& when the man
charges the tank
we are not afraid
until the crash
blood & fish
running out
a shark thrashing
in the shallows
an avalanche
of species
hyperventilating
at our feet
the man drowning
& bleeding
in the aquarium
the bottom feeders
still feeding
as if nothing
happened
always the last
to hear the news
watery joesoaps
waving to each other
like there was
no tomorrow

ii

in the money museum
they have the skeleton
of a fund manager
his joints are wired
like nature
he articulates perfectly
above our heads
he swings
like a fiscal acrobat

over the banks
of carefully conserved
legal tender
folding money
& plastic money
& specie
but at night he weeps
the pity of it
tender rain
on the glass screens
his weird sobbing
his bones tinkling
the derivatives he cries
the private equity
the toxic trades
the mega-bonus
what a life I had
when capital was young
& wall street
was disneyland
or woolworths anyway

ii

in the sex museum
online chat
runs continuously
& webcam girls
in continuous loops
only the most
famous cybersex
& iconic moneyshots
& extreme
& fetish
a brutal rape
a gangbang
public sex

& upskirts
household names
of depravity
in stills
& stilettos
stud cocks
preserved in brine
fully erect
with scales
in metric
& imperial
(≥9 inches)
there are always
teens near you
these lovelies
horny & waiting
in the sex
museum
entrance requires
a paypal account
register now
or enter
the password
this is what
freedom means
happy endings
you can
see everything
we wanted
to see
in the sex
museum

iv

in the science
museum
you are perfectly safe
ever surface
is sterile
& the artificial
staff have been
vetted carefully
every gesture
is protected
by copyright
nobody here owns
the knowledge
teamwork
is what works
& each unit
of the team is
dispensable

& here in this humble
kilner jar
a kitchen-level
device is a minor
miracle of globalization
the probable cure
for ebola virus
& cancer
& tax evasion
although at present
it mainly contains
just ebola virus
as you know
the cure usually
contains the disease

On a line of Beckett's misheard

a mouse clicks
in the untidy study

MacGowran's high-fidelity
grinding down the wires

in sentences
of noughts & ones

my words are my peers
turn as I may

there is no stepping outside
everything is here

the complete works
& what does not work

& the works outing
failures

language is everything
or all we have

& a ten year storm
pushes the trees away

& used leaves race
point to pointlessness

our frazzled planet
approaching nought

The time I spend

the time I spend
making something
feel unmade

fallen together
like an old tool-box
everything there

in its own way
too well-used
half worn away

& as a whole
disorganised
& then below

everything
is I know
one matchless

well-honed blade
a centre-punch
or a chisel

perfectly adapted
to my purpose
if I could find it

On formally undecidable propositions

for David Means

no one believes Cassandra
& Lazarus keeps mum
the sibyl at Cumæ
burned six of her nine books
bargains at the price

disbelief
silence
incompleteness
these are the instruments
we do what we can

5 places in County Cork

i Tiraneering

in the country of iron
iron men walk out of the hills
for the messages
(smoked bacon

& tobacco)
their hearts
are pig-iron   break
with the tap of a hammer

in autumn everything
is rust & rain
bracken burning
fresh from the forge

ii Tirnaspideoga

this is the yard of Bergen-Belsen
the ice-road to Leningrad
& the deck of my uncle's ship
on the Murmansk run
hardship hardens the soul

in the country of the robin
they pick the ground over
hopelessly
forever winter without snow
a hard frost defeats everything

lives turn on certain warm days
spring driving the chain
figures in a bleak landscape
seemingly immobile
are actually moving in small ways

iii   Leabasheeda

is no bed of roses
old women know
where they lie
is what they made

it could be Iraq
on a wet day
if they get wet days
a shithouse in a gale of wind

you wouldn't quarter
animals here
the draft under the door
the rain down on the fire

that old bastard she married
putting his false teeth
in the kettle
for the night

iv   Tiravan

Tiravan is exactly
in the middle
but of what
nobody knows anymore

some say the fields
stretch on either side
infinitely
to the edge

of whatever
there is an edge of
the universe
or the way we see it

& some say
that is a contradiction
in terms
& there is no edge

& therefore no middle
instead it is equidistant
from any two places
you might want to be

a spiritual centre
so to speak
a place where nothing
means anything

v   *In Lisavaird*

the poets holed up
for the last stand
writing their testaments
bitching

behind the earthworks
the food ran out
& then the paper
& someone poisoned the well

the last of the whiskey
went on the naming ceremony
the poet's fort
they're eating each other in there now

The easy way

you could take the easy way once in a while he said
but I know the road
went down that way once a long time ago
saw laurels stick ceramic tongues
& in the under-emptiness
there were opportunities for hiding & watching
but not touching or feeling
the laurel smell is still in my head even here
also empty cottages & so forth
some kind of racial memory
of famine running
through it like a dry course
but having gone down that road
I'm thinking
just because it's easy

maybe there's a better way
along the foreshore at low tide
where the ocean washes
drowned airmen
& snuffed chandlery
old nets that have escaped their victims
buoys grown tired of being marked men
dead life-jackets waving say
kapok kapok
the tortured bladder-wrack
a dry sewer-mouth
stitched into the genitals of a Holm oak
someone's lost or stolen knickers
crowning a thorn-tree
you could take the easy way
once in a while he said

a ship's rumbling engine
propagates in the sound
& also in the uncertain ground
& a tide rising behind
cuts off my retreat
now I remember the storage tanks
on the aluminium island
& also the water filmed in Technicolor
o ill-mannered refinery
leaking refined & crude
out at the end of the slow jetty
a tanker shows its crusty private parts
my plimsolls sink
you could take the easy way once in a while he said
you could take the easy way

& there childhood remains
my last good day
the memory of ease
& liberty
sometime one mid-afternoon
no trick of the light
no sleight of sky
soundlessly
without as much
as a by your leave
a silent winter set in me
bones setting like sudden ice
a rigorous fever calling
twice a day
it's been hard times since
& as it happens
there was never an easy way

Behind a hospital somewhere in Italy

carrion of self
in pits of hospital waste
used mattresses
discarded sharps
still the scintilla
of human blood
the dream-colour
of lips nipples penistips
this is the throat of the world
& we pour down
our toxic secondhand
second hands
& kidneys
& pre-used foetuses
& ex-brains
I am not well at all
but I listen to doom
on the carbon jukebox
like listening to Bartók
as if the evening
of our testicular trading
were not already
upon us
the new world order
already passé
in the groves of north London
where carbon trading
happens on a bendy-bus
between shortfalls of small change
& short-taken accountants
selling each other bets
on bets on longshots
or on the bourse
where nobody knows

anythinganymore
because the calculations
have a half-life of a million years
& there is not enough energy
in the planet
to power the indictment
I am not well at all
but I go out into hinterlands
like a firecracker
I follow the intellectual piper
into any old mountain
like a rat or a child
& when I go in
I stay in for as long
as I can hold my breath
I come out ten years later
older & wiser
unable to stand the light
with a compromised
immune system
& a bad chest
I am not well at all
but I take steroids
& marijuana
when I can get it
& as much fine wine as possible
& I take my wife to the pictures
or she takes me
we who resent happy endings
because this old ball of shit
rolling round in its diurnal course
is all that we have
no stepping off
no nextstopmindthegap
don't forget to touch
your oyster
I am not well at all

& standing here
on the tip
the black ash of the soul
that murder made
representing what we do
to each other
in the simple metaphor
of a discarded cannula
I feel light-headed
empty-hearted
& alone
I am not well at all
& none of us are
who drank our hearts out
in the smoke-filled bars
& ballad lounges
& drove our drunken rallies
round the back-road girls
who didn't want to hear about us
our very own
long night of the underman
who grew up
& became overman
entrepreneurs
& property developers
enveloping fields in cladding
inventing an empty
language for the flat world
driving secondhand
Mercedes
& bottle-blond
trophy women
who fucked
once upon a time
the secondhand
clock of the world
like there were no yesterdays

Nice

I hear the seagulls barking
in the bay of angels
soaring above the city
to sit on Garibaldi's head
they shit elsewhere

this sea has its way
of eating the continent
from the inside out
fishless   full of women
breasts sweetly sere

whose cuntsmell floats
serene with suntan oil
musk of the mare nostrum
they lie on the beach
legsspread

& the sun enters
& they gather things
in the late evening
who knows where to go
the kingsize doubles
of the Negresco
or a click-clack
in a high-rise in L'Ariane

the gulls pick over
the scrofulous sand
& the beery moon
rises on Americans
intent on experience
before turning in

Earthquake 1

*Every native of the city carries in him
the memory of an earthquake*

Pablo Neruda, *Memoirs*

in too many senses I know
& do not know
but there are no stories
later than the catastrophe
they prophecy

since there are waves in water
there are waves in earth air & fire
& all share
in the one power
which is to surprise the unprepared

carry the memory of the sine wave
the law of conservation
of angular momentum
as tree-rings carry the summer
furies await the forgetful

The frost performs its secret ministry

out of a clear sky a frozen landscape falls
a paradigm of fields & trees
as smooth as fibreglass
there is no sound
time to consider the extinction
of the species & how the universe
will cope without us

this is how the end of the world will be
white & definite & exactly as we imagine it
the perfection of our ambitions
at the end of everything a bird will sing
staking one last claim on the atlas
the liquid consonants propagating
unhindered like a new kind of life

Aeneas & the dead

i   *Cumæ: thunderstorm*

the place has a bad name
& Averno is the door
to the underworld
watch your step
in the fields of fire
it's a long way down

your father attends
in the waiting place
confused by the bustle
the efficiency
where is the handshake
the welcome

it's a war zone
on a Friday night
the punctured lungs
the ruined eyes
the broken limbs
the poisoning

he wants long-sight
to see you coming
not exactly a rescue
but head & shoulders
above the restless crowd
to say goodbye

ii   Capo Miseno: Aeneas finds Misenus drowned

I know those birds
wheeling over chalk
birds of love
lead me to the dark
a poisoned lake
in the fields of fire

the son of wind
the cry of brass
your haughty song
challenged the gods
the hoarse sea
was your applause

pitch-pine oak & fir
will be your pyre
we name this place for you
& hurry by
this windy cape
these straits

Naples, island ferry

for Salvatore Costagliola di Fiore

go to the Molo Bevorello he said
pay at the little kiosk
there will be a ferry waiting

do not fall asleep on the seat in the shade
or you will visit each island in turn
& come back to the same place

when you wake you will have passed
through the past the present & future
& you will have to begin again

I see him standing on the quay
men are taking boxes out of cars
passing them into the darkness

someone is waiting for us to disembark
when we step ashore we will enter another world
I feel the shiver of the crossing

everything will be the same
& different on this shore
when we turn to look back at the ship

we will be looking outwards
though the same crossing will be there
we will notice the uncertain light

a ripple in the air
a turn in the tide of the fluid we breathe
the world is always novel from an island

A white bird over Ischia

i

a white bird over Ischia
like tinfoil trapped in turbulent air
Naples behind
in the world's forgotten future

ii

the scirocco comes in from Africa
under cover of darkness
an unwelcome guest
the people unite against it

iii

a dog barks in Via Paradiso
he knows who the enemy is
the wind whistles in the orange groves
last year's fruit turning to stone

iv

fireworks popping
like frantic gunfire
somewhere below Vesuvius
that old mountain
dangerous still

v

cock-crow in Via Solchiar
a million fires darken the air
they are burning in Gehenna

vi

in the early morning sand
bougainvillea petals
broken glass
shells buttons syringes
sea-horses drinking straws

vii

the south lies bound
in chains of dust
& blind in iron
hopeless patience
& the sea turns plastic
in its boundless grace

In Procida

i   *In Procida the shapes of roofs*

are never to be trusted
irregularity is the norm
but curves more than lines
hemispheres
half–cylinders

they reflect something essential
in the character
a willingness to adapt
to embrace
to deflect

you could call it
the problem of the south
this absence of hard facts
this uncertainty
re plane geometry

morning & evening
I hear the snore of the torch
tarring my neighbour's house
against who knows
what possible winter

& later in winter
returning again
I find a good roof
is not a sufficient defence
against the elements

ii   *In Procida the oranges*

are brighter than flowers
more profuse in winter
against the dark leaves

& come in three ways
those that are sweet
those that are sour

& the little mandarins
whose flesh shrinks
from the skin

like elderly scholars
whose case is less
than what it contains

& here the oranges
are colder than stones
& more profuse in winter

iii   *In Procida the streets*

are petrified
of lava
signs warn of danger
in case of damp

jet gleams
in February's rain
the memory
of an eruption

tongues wet
unexpectedly
& people wait
where they lie

like models
in alabaster
in better weather
they walk

the streets
forget nothing
catastrophe
the stones sing

Pliny the Younger's account of the eruption of Vesuvius

i

my uncle having left us
I bathed & went to supper & even slept
the trembling did not perturb me
a small thing where we were
but the night was a bad one

in the open yard we sat down
call it courage call it folly
but I read my Livy & made notes
though the light was doubtful
& our place was small

ii

with the frightened crowd
for whom every new alarm is an authority
they press & drive us headlong
the horses terrified
cannot be settled

even on level ground
we cannot stay the carriages
even with stones

& the sea rolled backward
leaving fish behind
a cloud of terrible note
divided by flashes
strange shapes of flame
like sheet–lightning but much larger
then darkness

not like a dark sky
or moonless night
a room shut up & all the lights out

the women the children
the men calling
some for parents
some for lovers
one cries for his own fate
hoping to die
one is afraid of dying

some petition the gods
some shouting
that there are gods no more
& that the last night
is upon the world

& some who by fictions
& inventions
supplement the evidence of our eyes
that our old Misenum is gone

iii

strange light
fire falling some way off
a snow of ash

did I not believe
that the whole world
was this calamity

I might have called too
(the stoic's consolation
that there is no help)

we pass an anxious night
between hope & fear
day brings the light of an eclipse

To a mountain

after the Italian of Eugenio Montale

often the worst of life I met
the brook gagging
the rucked leaf
the horse's brutal fall

I never knew goodness
except the miracle that reveals
divine indifference

it was the statue
in the somnolence of noon
the cloud
& the falcon's sudden stoop from it

The isogloss of the dead

After Carlo Levi's description of the Palerman catacombs

even in the city of the dead the women
lie down they say
the virgins & girls
hold the crown & the palm

the poor have their winding sheets
their bones
are their inscriptions
& the rich have fine clothes

all the generations
leaning like cornerboys
we almost expect them
to smoke

the dead also suffer
war's indignities
bombs have inflicted
barbarous wounds

lost arms lost legs
they have fallen over & over
& lie where they fell
families mixed that in life

never addressed a civil word
the rich have fallen
among the tenement poor
& are ill at ease

& the poor are scattered
out of their districts
they lie among strangers
speaking a strange dialect

reparation continues slowly
in the catacombs
only the finest surgeons are called
to restore the dead

only the most noted scholars
can hear & understand
the subtlety
& draw the isogloss

this street or that
which tenement even
among whose dialect
the dead might be at home

Virgil's tomb

is close to the station
through the motorway tunnel
in a little garden
they gave him land here
when he was evicted

close enough to the door
to the underworld
at Lake Averno
(several trains a day)
where Aeneas waits

looking up at the blue eye
that is water not sky
wanting to shake the hand
of the man
who made his name

in those days heroes
waited on poets
as if that made any difference
I was a poet once
oh you're welcome here

Earthquake 2

the days are shorter
today than yesterday
& it has nothing
to do with winter
the world is spinning
faster than before
the conservation
of angular momentum
transforms a catastrophe
in a shallow sea
into a universal truth
the days are shorter
today than yesterday

Terramurata, Easter mysteries

the commune refused
a luxury hotel
    for the old penitentiary
    where they make
styrofoam models for the mysteries

a dead Christ
like someone's father
    a virgin
    a Judas
all the dramatis personæ

as light as air
& they tell you the strange truth
    that the man
    who made the first Christ
was a murderer

Rome, starlings

& in the dusk
away over the Capitol
a million starlings
      wheeled in a column
     on an updraft
like fish in a tropical shoal
marvellous & ordinary

People fall asleep

for Oisín

& are awakened by a man from Mantua
or they find they have ploughed a furrow
out of which the dead walk
with outlandish requests

or sleeping in an orchard
the sweet smell of windfalls
wakes an unhappy ghost
all the past to play for

a cleric wakes from a dream of knives
to find the ground has shifted
sex power truth maybe
certainty impossible now

in a rented room at the Spanish Steps
death comes like ice
but dressed as azure-lidd'd sleep
never so terrible a night

I tucked my father in
for his last sleep & held his hand
we all did
we knew no lullabies

& it is the same thing in us
that is the quick & the dead
the one is shifted into the other
the sleeper turns to another world

Counterpoint

after the Italian of William Stabile

there are moments
precise moments in my evenings
in which I cease to be a man
I traverse seasons in a few minutes

I shed thoughts in spirals
lines of certainty   half-truths
as the wheat sheds its husk
at the first biting wind of September

but then you come   hair the russet of apples
& you gather just the husks
senses tuned to the thinnest frequency
the truth survives in counterpoint

Meeting at evening

the sun sank
& all the ways were dark
& we saw the edge of things
shrouded in dust & smoke

we ran our boat ashore
slaughtered a black ram
poured mead & wine & water
& the dead came

brides & virgins & girls
soldiers & young men
oh friend Elpenor
where have you been
we missed your oar

your voice in counsel
as one who dare not tell
he indicated by a simple gesture
that he had been in hell

Travels in an Italy of the mind

1

The directors of the railway company, I was told, formed the opinion that the appropriate response to the Global Economic Crisis was to reinstate a facility that had existed in the early days of the railroad but which had long been abolished by the development of what they considered a false & self-defeating sense of dignity among their poorer passengers, namely The Third Class Carriage, & immediately set about constructing such carriages in such a way that the very minimum of necessary accommodation was provided under a glass-perspex roof & with cheap plastic seats & no heating to speak of; however, to their chagrin, they discovered, on introducing the concept of a Third Class Carriage attached to the usual trains containing as usual First & Second Class carriages, that the part of the public to which the initiative was addressed was too poor to travel at all, thus, in effect, the very poorest were found to have a previously unheard of economic weight which rested in their ability not to choose & which rendered this particular well-meaning railway company a victim of the economic crisis to which they had hoped to respond with appropriate & well-intentioned measures. On discovering their mistake the company announced that *new measures were required.*

2

Two English tourists, a doctor & her architect husband, having eaten well & drunk a pint & a half of house wine at lunch, found themselves in the Piazza Dei Ferrari in Genoa & were so impressed by the equestrian statue of Giuseppe Garribaldi, that they immediately set off in high spirits, imitating people on horseback & applying invisible whips to their mounts towards the narrow lanes that lie in the direction of the port & which the locals all call caröggi in their Ligurian dialect which, as it happens, contains many letters & diacritical marks that are not part of the official Italian language which is really little more than Tuscan, & upon entering a particularly dark & narrow street found themselves at the entrance to a house which, by a strange coincidence, had a doorbell & a small brass plaque with their names inscribed on it. They could not account for this extraordinary *confrontation*, as they repeatedly termed it, & so they rang the doorbell. When there was no answer they concluded that the people who lived there, practising, as the brass plaque so helpfully informed them, the same professions of architect & medical doctor, & who had their exact names, were out.

3

In Monterosso the Russian writer who had come to find the house of Eugenio Montale went into a gelateria, as he said, to shelter from the cold. When he was asked by the owner, which they always do, not wanting people to clutter up their gelaterias, what he wanted, the Russian said Mint Flavour. There was no Mint Flavour so he expressed his regrets to the owner of the gelateria & left. He later told me that he already knew there was no Mint Flavour having first taken the precaution of examining the available flavours. When I asked him why he asked for that specific Mint Flavoured ice-cream, he told me that he did so in order to be polite.

4

Two men, travelling between Genoa & Milan on the so-called superfast train, each read a newspaper. The headline on one newspaper said: Mussolini insulted & no one does anything about it. The headline on the other newspaper said: Climate Change, USA & China compromise. Neither man looked up from his newspaper or spoke for the entire length of the journey which, having passed through several tunnels & valleys finally settled into the long passage through the Plain of Lombardy which everyone agrees is not worth seeing.

5

A communist eye-surgeon from Bologna told me that just the day before she had seen an unfortunate case. A man put a gun to his temple & pulled the trigger, intending to make an end of himself once & for all. The bullet severed the optic nerve behind his right eye & exited through the orbital lobe of his left eye completely *exploding* the eyeball & leaving him blind. After the shooting, she said, he was able to walk to the first aid station. When she saw him all he said was, I have such a terrible headache. She registered the cause of the trauma, she said, as *wilful blindness*.

6

An Irish computer engineer whom I met in Florence outside the church where, according to the exact English words on the plaque at the door, Dante *first clapped eyes on* Beatrice Portinari, whom he later made famous in his long poem & several shorter poems, & who travelled for a company that specialised in maintaining the atmosphere in museums at the correct level of temperature & humidity, a very delicate balance as he told me, & one upon which depended the very existence of many works of world-famous art, this Irish engineer told me that when he first began to travel in Europe he thought the bidet, which as he said, does not exactly advertise its purpose, was a foot-bath & he further told me that he was devastated when he discovered the truth not least because he was *a very bad case* of foot odour.

7

I once met a man outside the cubicle of the gents toilet in the Crawford Gallery in Cork who told me that the doors of the gents toilet cubicles were identical to those in the gents toilet cubicles in the Uffizzi Gallery in Florence, made of the same opaque green glass, but it was his opinion that the architect who had chosen to put the same opaque glass in the dividing walls between each of the cubicles, which was the case in the Crawford Gallery in Cork but not in the Uffizzi Gallery in Florence, had made a bad mistake & that it was, in fact, *an embarrassment to the city.*

8

A woman who in her youth had led a wild life, including travelling to India to obtain drugs, & sleeping with numerous people of both sexes as a result of reading Wilhelm Reich, & who was now a librarian & therefore a public servant, told me that she had spent so many years as a sponge diver in one of those places where they dive for sponges that her body had partaken of some of the qualities of sponges so that now, when the humidity was high, as today it was over 90% in Florence as witness the instrument in the instrument-maker's window at which she was looking when I spoke to her merely to ask directions to a restaurant, her body swelled up like a sponge & conversely when the humidity fell again she could spend twenty minutes at a time pissing it all away. This terrible flux had made her joints sponge-like & painful, especially her knees, ankles & hips, which in turn prevented her from getting around much & she had moved out of her *mansarda* in one of the better districts & was now living in a ground floor so-called studio that had cockroaches under the sink. Of course she had been to the hospital but one knows instinctively what such people will say when presented with an unusual case like this.

9

A Lebanese man & his young son were staring at a gap between the cobbles of the Street of the Well of the Crows. When I ask them what they were looking at they indicated a brightly coloured insect. The Lebanese man said the insect was a red palm weevil. Very dangerous, he said. He looked at me with appealing eyes but I was unable to help him. When I began to write down his observation in my notebook he ran away, his young son following him. I have since been unable to ascertain why the weevil was dangerous, although I believe he was telling the truth. I have not reported his observation to the authorities.

10

A woman who claimed to have been present in the Assize Court of Perugia at the time told me that the American girl who murdered her friend had been given twenty years. She was surprised that the girl cried because, as she said to me, if she had murdered her friend in The United States of America she would be sent to the electric chair. It seems therefore, I said, one should be careful about where one commits murder.

11

When the mountain erupted in 1944, the man from Naples told me, his father had a simple Kodak Brownie Junior with a meniscus lens that had been sent to him by a relative in New York & he had gone to photograph the strange effects of light which seemed to be, as his father expressed it to him, *distorted by the magnetic discharge from the fault*. In those days there was famine in Naples; people from the *bassi* were eating dandelions & cats, an American army blanket was worth a daughter's virginity & his family had to get everything on the black market. The images do not survive.

12

The man who played Rigoletto & the woman who played Gilda his daughter broke all historical precedent, something unknown in living memory, at the Genoa opera house by taking an encore *after the second act*. It was the talk of the town.

One half of the audience, those who voted for the Right, were shocked & hurt & felt let down by their beloved opera house, & the other half who voted for the ruling Communist Mayor were delighted at the discomfiture of their fellows.

13

A man was ejected from the Galleria Borghese because he lay on the floor in order, as he reported it to me, the better to see the ceiling. The gallery staff, who in any case had been following his antics, which they admitted to him were fascinating, on a closed circuit surveillance camera, ordered a security guard to remove him from the premises because, as he himself agreed & repeated to me, the exhibition was on the walls not the ceiling. He further told me that the security guard who brought him to the exit told him that the ceiling was, in fact, *the best thing in the place.*

14

A man from America with whom I had a glass of wine in the Taverna Romana in Via Monte dei Madonna told me that he could eat hamburgers every other day but he couldn't stand this Italian shit, these people, as he put it, who were always in your face. What was it that united an entire nation around what was, after all, as the man from America said, the kind of thing your pop liked? He spoke English with a pronounced Italian accent.

15

In Via Dei Spagnoli the man who made the fake antiques crossed the road to the tavernetta to buy his gnocchi alla gorgonzola because, as he told me, here was found the real Roman food than which, in his opinion, there was no better or healthier in the world.

16

The delegates to the UN Food & Agriculture conference somehow knew all the best places to eat & booked them out in advance so that people who usually ate there every day or even several days a week or for a treat maybe once a week because they could no longer afford to eat out so often, usually the smallest restaurants & trattorias which had the most particular dishes that were specialities of their particular riones, & these poor people were no longer able to eat there at all because they had been booked out by the Food & Agriculture crowd who of course had police escorts & arrived in SUVs with blacked out windows or Mercedes to what were the favourite eating places of the entire district, for example the Campo Marzio district. & so the locals had to eat in the tourist traps where the food was by general agreement execrable & not even fit for tourists & in fact gave Roman food a bad name, & the worst part was that they had to sometimes sit outside because the tourists who came in winter wanted to eat inside & therefore the local people of the Campo Marzio district for example had to watch the Food & Agriculture crowd being escorted by armed guards to eat in their favourite eating places. The delegates had, in the opinion of the local people, *an entirely different way of life*.

17

A man from Croatia told me that one can learn a great deal from how a people organises its maritime affairs & that the Venetians in the fifteenth century were the only people in the history of the world who mounted their cannons pointing over the sterns of their ships, & this was because by the time they already opened fire they were running away. The Venetians, in his considered opinion, were a very intelligent people & they were always working the numbers.

18

A woman I met in Cuma where I had gone to see the cave of
the Sybil, told me of a man of who had lived almost all his life
in the town of Pozzuoli, except for a brief stint with the
partisans after the rebellion of Naples. This autochthonous
partisan was widowed at the age of ninety & afterwards in the
confusion of his mind, as she said, he took up with a neighbour
who was ten years his junior & slept with her & the following
morning, wandering in a daze, as happens naturally enough in
these cases as much to the old as to the young, he found
himself knocking at the door of the priest; the priest brought
him in & the old man immediately told him that he had sex
with a woman of eighty years. Well, the priest said, being, as the
woman from Cuma told me, a new man & completely
unknown to the old man, as indeed the man was to the priest,
are you sorry for your sins. Sins?, the old man said. I don't
believe in any of that old shit, I'm a communist. Well what are
you telling me for so, the priest replied. Telling you, the old
man is reported as saying, I'm telling everybody.

19

A man on an island near Naples said to me that all the
important development works carried out in the area such as
the new marina or any of the very big houses & housing
projects were funded by the Camorra & they later paid the
politicians to pass them as safe. He made that sliding movement
between his index finger & thumb. He had seen on the TV
that in many low-lying areas of Ireland houses had been
flooded because these houses were built on the floodplain
against all professional advice &, as he himself had seen on the
same television report, conversely a large apartment building
on a hill had its roof blown off by the wind. He assumed that
all these developments were also *abusivi*.

20

It was reported by the press that the Prime Minister was attacked by a lunatic who broke his nose, his lip & two teeth with a model of the famous pseudo-gothic Cathedral of Milan. Afterwards the lunatic said he did not recognise himself in his actions. It was also reported by the press that another lunatic attacked the Pope in the basilica of St Peters, but the press did not mention whether this second violent lunatic, who was, in fact, a woman, had a model of the Cathedral of Milan, or a model of any other famous cathedral, or, in fact, any model at all, or even whether she recognised herself in her actions. If we can believe that the newspapers would faithfully report such a detail we must conclude that this female lunatic, or, at any rate, deranged woman, who leaped the rails, & who had actually leaped the same rails on a previous occasion with the same intention of attacking the pontiff, was empty-handed, although it was reported that *she wore, on both occasions, a red hooded jumper.*

About the Author

WILLIAM WALL is the author of two previous collections of poetry, four novels and a volume of short fiction. He has won numerous prizes including the Patrick Kavanagh Award and the Listowel Writers' Week prize and been nominated for many more, including the Man Booker Prize. He is a full-time writer and lives in Cork. More details from his website www.williamwall.eu

Photograph: Harry Moore